27 TIPS TO DEVELOP A SUPERPOWER MEMORY

Varsha
Anna
Cyriac

GOODWILL'S

27 TIPS TO DEVELOP A SUPERPOWER MEMORY

KAY WHITE

GOODWILL PUBLISHING HOUSE
B-9, Rattan Jyoti, 18 Rajendra Place
New Delhi - 110 008

Published by:
GOODWILL PUBLISHING HOUSE
B-9, Rattan Jyoti, 18, Rajendra Place
New Delhi-110 008 (INDIA)
Phone: 5750801, 5755519
Fax: 5763428.

First Published 1997

Price Rs. 45/-

Laser Typeset at: Computer Corner, New Delhi.

Printed at Kumar Offset Printers Ph. : 2213315

CONTENTS

Introduction

"You don't remember anything!" since childhood you had been hearing this complaint from your mother when you used to forget something for which you were expressly sent to the neighbourhood market. Now, your wife tells you the same thing when you forget the entire shopping list thrust in your pocket by her before you left for office! You dread the day when you would become old and perhaps become amnesiac.

You were a brilliant student, now you are a responsible officer. Still you used to forget and still keep on forgetting that wretched shopping list. You wonder how you forget again and again the very thing which your wife tells you not to forget. You are ashamed, you are perplexed, and then you accept the reality of the thing, shrug shoulders and forget the whole episode to be repeated again and again in the future.

You are in a party and you see somebody who smiles and warmly advances towards you with out-stretched hands. You vaguely remember the face but are unable to recognize the person. Worst still, you have no clue to his name. He asks about your wife, your family, your work and you keep on replying to him absent-mindedly frantically searching in your memory for some idea of his identity!

You like to play cards but your game has never risen above the mediocre. Your partner is always cross with you for playing wrong cards because you do not remember which cards have been played and which are still held in the hands. **Sometimes you even play your King forgetting that the Ace is still held by somebody!**

People talk of past years. **How much it rained then, how much potato cost, how sweet the mangoes used to be, how much exactly was their salary, on which date they had come to the city to join their Service.** You wonder how one could remember such details. You don't even remember your date of joining the service!

"Can you tell me which road is this?" This! Hum . . . This goes to the office. But the name? You don't know it! In fact you don't know which roads you take to reach the office. You know the way, but not the name of the roads.

Your circle of friends is limited, yet each time you have to telephone them you have to find out the number from the diary. If somebody tells you to dial some number you have to ask it again because before you dial the first three digits you forget the remaining ones!

If you are a student the question of memory becomes very important for you. How to memorize the lessons; the names and dates of history; the equations of maths; physics, and chemistry; quotations in literature.

The problem is now getting serious. You forget and misplace things and important papers. The same is happening at the office. You are even forgetting appointments and forget what your boss wanted you to do.

You have an important talk to deliver. **You had memorized by rote the entire speech but as soon as you stand to speak you**

have clean forgotten it! What an embarrassment!

It seems a nightmarish life. Are you normal or not? Is it your problem or of practically everybody's? Can something be done about it?

—KAY WHITE

I

Mechanism of Memory Tips

Human mind is sometimes compared to computer or rather computer is sometimes compared to human mind. Mind, however, is infinitely superior to computers as computers cannot think for themselves. In other words computers have no intelligence. The ultimate aim of computer scientists may be to make a computer which has human intelligence.

Like human-beings computers also remember and this capacity of remembering is also called memory. First of all computers remember the basic or fundamental instructions coded into it which enable it to function. This memory may be compared with our intuitions and instincts and perhaps the way we interpret the sense data. Computers have, however, another memory. If we type or draw something on computer and then give it a command called 'save' our typed material or drawn picture goes into computer's memory and we can bring it back or recall it as and when we desire. If, however, before we had opportunity to save it, suddenly the power goes off or we switch off the computer, normally the material is lost for ever. Now-a-days most of the computers (programmes) automatically save the material. We can erase the saved material, sometimes it is accidentally lost, sometimes we may not be able to recall it because we may forget where we have saved it. If we understand well the process involved in the saving of material on computers we may better manage it. Similarly, if we understand well the process of human memory well we may better remember. To describe fully the process involved in human memory is not our main concern here. So, we will limit ourselves only to its practical side.

1

ORDER YOUR MIND TO REMEMBER

Memory can not recall something which it has not registered in the first place or registered imperfectly. Most of the failures of the recall come into this category. You don't recall a friend's face or name; you cannot name the roads and describe the buildings on your way to the office; you forget the entire shopping list or some items out of it. The fault may be that you never noticed them in the first place. Did you see the man and heard his name clearly who has just been introduced to you. Do you read the names of the roads and buildings when you pass by them? Do you pay attention when your wife is counting the items on your shopping list? Perhaps not. So, **how you expect to remember a thing which you did not pay attention to and note, in other words did not consider worth remembering in the first place?**

2

DO GOOD FILING, INDEXING AND RECORDING JOB

In a good office correspondence is filed properly. Files may be opened in various ways depending on the nature of work, but the most common criteria is subject. Files on similar subject may be opened under a common Head or Sub-Head and accordingly filed in a given drawer or cabinet. Good filing is essential for fast and efficient retrieval. If number of files is large they may be indexed. Old files may be recorded and kept at a separate place which may be away from the immediate work-place.

In computers also material is saved in files. Files on the same subject are grouped together in a separate Directory or Sub-Directory. These files may be retrieved easily, acted upon and again kept back.

In many respect mind works like computer. It is, therefore, very necessary that after giving mind the order to note something properly and memorize it, we may help mind to file it properly too. In most of the memory matters quick retrieval is very essential. We must recall the name of the person immediately on meeting him or her. We must keep on talking and recalling subsequent speech on a speaking assignment. It would, therefore, not do to rummage around and come up with the relevant file. We must have instant recall and for this proper filing is essential.

3

DON'T BE CONFUSED

Improper filing leads to confusion. It is not enough to file similar facts together. Each separate fact must exist as distinct as well. We must also be able to cross-reference.

What happens when we forget names and faces? Suppose in a marriage reception dinner we are introduced to five persons. We know that this is a casual social meeting, perhaps we will never meet again, there does not seem to be anything common between us. So, our mind does not record even. We forget immediately.

Forgetting names of known persons and colleagues is another matter. Perhaps we are in the habit of dumping all the names in a common file without noting each name as distinct and associating it with the proper face, occupation, and distinctive personality characteristics. When we want to recall the name we rummage into the file containing names and in a haste do not come up with the proper name. Perhaps we come up with the occupation or personality characteristics, but since we have not made firm links, the name eludes us.

4

TAKE THE HELP OF SUB-CONSCIOUS MIND

In psychology we learn that our deep rooted fears, anxieties, and wishes remain in latent form in our sub-conscious mind and profoundly affect our life at crucial times. These are pushed back to sub-conscious mind by the conscious mind so that they do not interfere in day-to-day living of the person.

Similarly, conscious mind puts unnecessary information in the sub-conscious mind so that conscious mind is not cluttered unnecessarily, but at the same time the information is available if needed. In this sense mind never forgets anything. In fact now in most of the computer programmes also when we delete/erase a file it is actually not deleted/erased but put in a separate place from where it can be retrieved.

Sub-conscious mind is, however, not under our direct command. Also since it contains much-much larger amount of material in it than the conscious mind it searches slowly So if we are unable to recall where we put something, we may politely ask our sub-conscious mind to recall it. Now it is not necessary that the information is necessarily in the sub-conscious itself: it may be in the conscious mind. Sub-conscious mind starts searching for the missing information and in most cases after a good night's sleep it comes up with the reply by the morning.

5

GIVE FACTS CONTEXT/ BACKGROUND

We do not see a thing in isolation but in context and against a background. We see a tree together with all the things around it. Similarly, we do not read words in isolation, but within a given context and background which make the words meaningful. Since normally in life we do not experience anything in isolation mind forgets isolated facts in no time. To keep it in mind we must give it the necessary context.

It is this context/background which enables us to remember countless facts about our family and friends. We remember stories because they have the necessary context and background.

6

CONVERT FACTS INTO YOUR OWN LANGUAGE/ FORMAT

Mind does not remember things as we see them but converts them to suit it. For example, we see things two dimensionally (because the image formed on our retina is two dimensional) yet mind remembers the world as three dimensional. Stranger than this is the fact that when we see a table we hardly see its four legs or its back side but the mind supplies the missing information and we remember a table with four legs. Some things mind remembers easily, others not.

We can remember an entire poem in our language, but not remember even a word in unknown language or a nonsense world. It is easy to remember the word **ELEPHANT** and the letters it is made up of. But a nonsense word like **TNAHPELE** is impossible to remember (**unless, of course, we note that it is elephant written in reverse order).**

Similarly, mind has its own language and preferences and to remember something we must put our information in the format most suitable for the mind. Some of these formats we will be learning latter. We may mention a few of them here. They are—**symmetry, linkage, interesting, concrete, emotional,** and **visual** etc.

7

UNDERSTAND THE WHOLE

We have seen that our mind stores the information in holograms that is as a whole. It is, therefore, easy to remember something if we understand the whole of it and can see it as a whole in our mind's eye.

Suppose you are given the story of **Thomas Hardy's Tess** in question and answer in such a way that the answers in a haphazard way give the entire story of the novel. It will be still very difficult to piece out the story from these answers and it will be even more difficult to remember them. However, if you have read the whole novel carefully once not only you will remember it but it will be easy to remember the answers to various questions mentioned above.

8

BREAK THE INFORMATION INTO ITS COMPONENTS PARTS

It is, however, necessary to break a complex whole to break into its constituent parts to understand and remember well.

To understand and remember well the mechanism of a motor-car we may study its various systems, to understand the organisation of a company we may draw its hierarchy chart, to understand an assembly line process we may draw its flow chart. To memorize a lengthy material we may sub-divide it into various Headings and Sub-Headings.

9

MAKE A MIND-MAP

We generally arrange material in a sequential and arranged manner. Mind, however, does not arrange facts in such an orderly fashion. It helps to remember things if we arrange our ideas in a branching tree or river fashion. Here ideas are not arranged in neatly written or drawn schematic model but they look on paper like a web.

II

Psychological Tips

Memory is in the mind! In fact nearly everything is in the mind. Many philosophers believe that nothing exists outside our minds—meaning that there is no physical world out there, it is only our mind which gives us an illusion of it. Even if we do not go that far it is still true that what we see in the world depends on our mind and its attitude. Not only our emotions and feelings give colour to our view of the world and life, they also subtly affect our health, capacity, and resolve.

It is therefore important that we are psychologically

ready for our programme of memory improvement. Now-a-days even sports persons and top executives are given psychological help to improve their performance.

Before we try to offer solutions for forgetfulness, and study the systems to improve the memory, it is necessary to learn something about memory itself.

An adult human brain contains around 11,000 million brain cells or neurons. At the centre of the neuron is the cell body from which issue forth tentacles which themselves branch out into even more tentacles. Neurons are inter-connected through these tentacles. The number of permutations and combinations of the inter-connection of these 11,000 million neurons is thus almost infinite. So, the capacity of the brain is almost limitless and we may say that it records everything which happens in our life.

There are different theories about the actual process involved in this recording. This may be electrical or this may be chemical (RNA) or both. This recording was thought to be localised for different type of functions of the brain (learning, music, perception, and motor activity etc.). However, there is evidence also for the suggestion that even if memory is recorded at different places in the brain according to its contents at every place it could also be in the form of a 'whole'. This is very much like a **hologram** (literally, whole record). A hologram is like a photograph taken with the help of laser beam. If viewed under the same laser light it looks like a three dimensional image. If the glass plate on which this hologram is developed is broken into pieces then each piece, if viewed under the same laser light contains the whole picture. We may also compare the memory to the recording on a video cassette or computer diskette.

What are the things our memory stores? Of course, mainly the sense data. Whatever we see, hear, smell, touch, taste, and also learn, imagine, etc. We do not, however, record much during our state of sleep. Why? Because our senses hardly notice anything while we sleep. Similarly, we may wander through the city without noticing anything and, therefore, without having any precise memory later on.

From this sketchy description of memory we may get some tips ahead for memory improvement.

10

CAN AND ABLE—YOU CAN DO IT AND BETTER THAN OTHERS

The first tip to be successful in any thing to believe that you can do it and you are able to do it. Fortunately, in the matter of memory it is not difficult to believe that you and do it and you are able to do it. God has given you such a marvellous brain that even today scientists are not able to fully understand it let alone duplicate it. This brain is capable of remembering each and every thing of your life.

If you want to learn swimming or driving or music, the first thing to understand is that if persons otherwise very inferior to you could do it you could also—If an illiterate can swim, drive or play music surely you could also do it; if somebody younger than you, less intelligent, or less smart can do it you can also do it. Similarly, if illiterate, less educated, less intelligent person seem to have better memory surely you can and are able to develop your memory. You have the advantage that you have decided to improve your memory and are reading this book!

11

I WILL RESOLVE TO DO IT AND NOW

Of course even if you can and are able to do it you may still fail unless you resolve to do it. Without will-power nothing is possible—and by willing even mountains could be moved!

But nothing in life comes easily and things which come easily are not worth much. A scientist, a writer, and a musician, may devote his or her entire life to the chosen field before being successful. Other things, like maintaining good health, may be simple in the sense that they may require following a few simple truths, but still they may also require a life-long commitment. Keeping good health may require good eating, living, and exercise habits. In themselves these may not require a persons full-time and energy but require him or her constantly practising the rules of good health.

Similarly, our aim in this book is not to be obsessive about memory. We do not want to be memory freak. Fortunately, we can practice memory improvement tips without devoting time exclusively on it but making it a way of life.

Many things in life we are never able to do though we constantly wish to do them. We keep on postponing them for next day, next week, next month, next year .... I will leave smoking, I will start Yoga, I will visit a hill station, I will learn music, the list is unending but we invariably fail to even start to do what we so desperately wish to do.

So, **resolve to improve your memory and start to do so right now. Read on and practice.**

12

GET RID OF INFERIORITY COMPLEX

God is just and impartial. He has made all human-beings equal but different. Especially in the case of human brain he has made it so infinitely complex and full of capacity that not only it is capable of extra ordinary memory there is no real difference between the capacity of one brain and another. Infinities even if they may not be equal are never compared and there is no lesser or greater infinity.

So, there is no basis of thinking that one's brain is inferior to another's. Human nature, however, is strange. In many things we willingly belittle ourselves but in others not. I may accept that I am suffering from cold or headache or some other long term disease but I will never accept that I have character flaws of anger, fear, or jealousy. Similarly, I may readily say that my memory is terrible, but I shall never accept that I'm less intelligent than Solomon!

But if you want to improve your memory get rid of the inferiority complex that your memory is inferior to anybody else.

Remember you are not alone who thinks he has a memory problem. Nor is it confined to men only, women also do forget—but, of course, not the shopping list, they are even capable of adding some new items to it! If you are not alone with this problem. It could not be such a sin. In fact, though this could not be a great solace, most of the great thinkers, scientists, philosophers, and writers etc. have been known for their forgetfulness. Some are even reputedly credited with the perplexing question **"who are you?"** to their wives when they met them in their moments of forgetfulness! In fact forgetfulness is natures way of clearing the decks, as it were, of the human memory of the useless information. Our mind keeps on doing this.

13

BE CONFIDENT

Once you know that you can and are able, are determined, and have got rid of the inferiority complex you will be supremely confident of your memory.

Without self-confidence nothing can be accomplished. Confidence is required not only to beat your opponent in a competition like a tennis match, it is also required to overcome one's inner fear and doubts. It requires confidence to jump into the water to swim when there is nobody around to help, it requires confidence to go on the roads to drive alone after the driving lessons are completed, and it requires confidence to face the audience to deliver a lecture without notes.

If confidence makes possible to happen, fear and doubts make it impossible to happen. All negative tendencies are self-destructive. Each time you doubt and hesitate you give your mind a message which mind interprets as a normal command and acts in a way that the doubts are justified. If you think that you cannot remember a fact or figure, it gives a command to mind—"**Forget this!**" Mind, accordingly, brings into play all the devices available to it to forget even though as a matter of routine the fact or figure has been properly registered in the mind!

14

FIGURE OUT YOUR OWN PROBLEMS

Confidence and resolve, howsoever necessary and important, cannot by themselves give you super memory. The most powerful and modern motor-car cannot run without its key, or petrol, or tyres.

You may have an excellent memory but it may also be true that you may be forgetting names and faces, facts and figures, and quotations. Without figuring out the problem it cannot be solved. Most of us must have gone through the embarrassing situation of thoroughly checking an electrical equipment without being able to repair it till somebody pointed out that there was no electricity or the electric switch itself was faulty!

You must therefore embark upon a thorough introspection. **What do you usually forget?** Do you forget everything or only names and faces? Do you forget numbers? Do you forget the answers in the examination hall or speech on the dais? What could be the reason of your forgetting particular type of information? Perhaps you forget the names because when introduced you hardly pay attention to it; may be you forget faces because you do not remark the distinctive features; perhaps you cannot remember numbers because you have a psychological fear of them; you do not recall answers in the examination halls because you have tried to learn by rote without understanding anything; you perform poorly as a speaker because you become too nervous. Once you know what is your weakness and the probable cause of it, you are well on the road to overcoming your memory problem.

15

ORDER YOUR MIND TO REMEMBER

You must have heard it said of a number of things that it is a good servant but bad master. For example, science is a good servant but bad master. Similarly, our brain is a good servant but bad master. We must discipline and command our mind. On its own mind keeps on either forgetting or putting into its attic room most of the information. This it does not to clutter itself with unnecessary information. But generally it is mind itself which decides what is important and what is not. When it decides on its own that names or faces or numbers are not important and they are best forgotten, we tend to forget them.

So, we must order our mind to remember what we want it to remember. Tell it what you consider important. Order it to remember it. Command it to take your prior permission before it forgets something or stores it in its attic room.

16

REMEMBER THE CAPACITY OF YOUR MIND IS ALMOST INFINITE

We have seen how complex the human mind is. In fact the extraordinary memory power exhibited by some persons is mind boggling. **S.** (so described in research papers) remembered a 50 digits matrix in 3 minutes and could tell it in any order even after years later! He could also memorize any type of material even scientific formulae and poems in languages he did not know. Professor Aitken could recall the value of II **(*pie* = approx. 22/7) up to 1,000 decimal places,**

both forward and backward! In some of the tests he recalled the test material perfectly even after 27 years!

III

Mnemonics Tips

Mnemonic is both the art and science of improving memory as well as a system for this.

We all use some of its devices without being consciously aware of it. Abbreviations and mathematical formulae can also be said to be mnemonics.

These are handy for remembering series of facts and figures each member of which is logically unconnected with the others, and are, therefore, difficult to remember. Examples of such series may be a shopping list, a telephone number, random numbers, and things. You may master them easily and become the master of super-memory. Some of these devices are mentioning ahead.

17

LINK THE ITEMS THROUGH A SHORT STORY

Suppose you have to remember the following list—

COAT

CAR

FOOTBALL

LAUGH

ICE-CREAM

AIR

HORSE

SWORD

GREEN

TOMATO

Try howsoever hard to remember this list you would make at least one mistake each time you try to repeat it. Now link all them—

> I was to go to a party. I put on my best COAT and drove in my CAR. On the way I passed a FOOTBALL field out side which a joker was making people LAUGH and selling ICE-CREAM. My car had a puncture and there was nobody to fill in the AIR. I rode a HORSE. At the gate the guard had a long SWORD. The hostess was all dressed up in GREEN and offered me a glass of TOMATO juice.

I bet now you will never forget the list!

Some tips on the image making in the Link system are—

> Make images involving yourself. Make predominantly visual image but try to involve

all senses. Make solid images of abstract ideas. Make simple and logical sequences but exaggerate the sizes and distort the features to the point of absurdity of the objects involved so that they become easy to remember. Use humorous, colourful, and, if it suits you sexual imagery.

18

LINK THE ITEMS WITH FAMILIAR PLACES

In the **Link System** you linked the images in a story form sequentially. In the **Place or Peg System** try to link the items to a set series of objects or places familiar to you. Suppose the lay-out of your house and the ten most important things, from our point of view of applying present system, in it are—

DRAWING ROOM

SOFA

TV

MUSIC SYSTEM

STAIRS

BED

COMPUTER

STUDY TABLE

WALL CLOCK

BATH ROOM

Now you can imagine entering your house and finding the drawing room all done in red, a horse sitting in your sofa, watching a football match on the TV, and listening to Madonna. A car is moving upstairs and a book is lying open on your bed. On your computer Windows programme is running and a letter is lying on your study table. Wall Clock is showing the time ten hours and water is running in the bath-room.

This helps you to remember following things in the correct order—

RED

HORSE

FOOTBALL

MADONNA

CAR

BOOK

WINDOW

LETTER

TEN

WATER

19

LINK THE ITEMS WITH NUMBER-SOUND

This system is based on words which rhyme with the numbers 1-10—

1. SUN
2. SHOE
3. TREE
4. DOOR
5. HIVE
6. STICKS
7. HEAVEN
8. GATE

9. WINE

10. HEN

To remember a list of ten items in sequence we associate the items with the corresponding things in above list making vivid, exaggerated, and absurd images to make them easy to recall. A typical story line could be—

A man sweating in the **sun** in a boat shaped like a **shoe** sailing in the river on the bank of which there is a **tree** with dollar bills growing on it. The man opens a **door** on which a snake is moving towards a **hive** in which fairies are living. The man uses a **stick** to catch fish. Elephants fall down from the **heaven**, the boat enters the mouth of a whale which opens like a **gate**. Inside a lady is drinking **wine** and a **hen** is reading a book.

The things in the list are—**man, boat, dollar, snake, fairy, fish, elephants, whale, lady,** and **book.** Of course, you can remember the things in sequence without creating a story line individually linking the items with sun, shoe, etc.

20

LINK THE ITEMS WITH NUMBER-SHAPE

This system is similar to the **Number-Sound System,** but here instead of using the sounds of the numbers as cue to the pegs, you use the shape of the numbers as your pegging things. The numerals look like—

1. FLAG POLE
2. READY TO STRIKE SNAKE
3. BOW (BUTTOCKS For Sexual Imagery)
4. SAIL OF A BOAT
5. SCYTHE
6. HANGING LIGHT BULB

7. SPADE
8. HOUR GLASS (BUXOM BEAUTY For Sexual Imagery)
9. BALLOON
10. BOY WITH A WHEEL

21

LINK THE ITEMS WITH ALPHABET-SOUND

Here every letter of the alphabet is linked with a word of similar initial sound, as is done for numbers in **Number-Sound System**—

A	ACE	B	BEE
C	SEA	D	DEAN
E	EEL	F	EIFFEL (TOWER)
G	JEANS	H	HATCH
I	EYE	J	JAY
K	CAKE	L	ELM
M	EMBASSY	N	ANT
O	OWL	P	PEA

Q	QUEUE	R	ARM
S	ESSAY	T	TEA
U	YOUTH	V	VJ
W	W-C	X	X-RAY
Y	WINE	Z	ZOO

This system not only enables you to memorize up to 26 items in sequence but may also help you to recall a sequence of letters like APTHLM. You have only to link up ACE, PEA, TEA, HATCH, ELM, and EMBASSY.

22

LINK THE ITEMS WITH PHONETICS OR NUMBER-LETTER

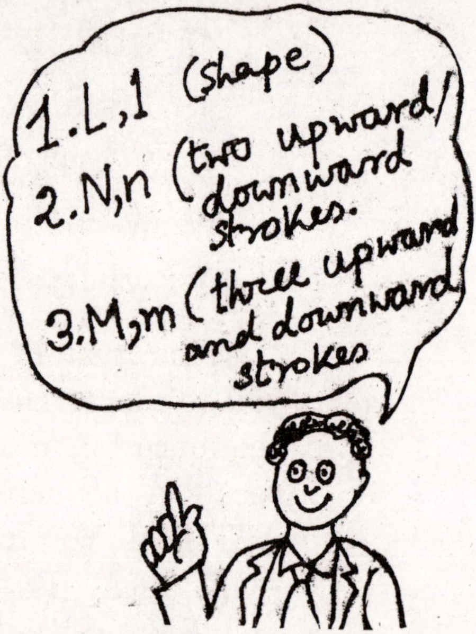

In this system the numbers 1 to 10 are linked with ten letters of the alphabet. The linkage can be made taking into consideration any of the particularity of shape, sound, or a combination of these. Below is a suggested pegging system in which we have left out vowels (because these we will supply when making out words) and some other unimportant letters (since in any case we have only ten numbers to which letters can be linked)—

1. L, 1 (shape)

2. N, n	(two upward/ downward strokes)
3. M, m	(three upward/ downward strokes)
4. R, r	(sound)
5. C, K, c, k,	(shape)
6. S, s, sh	(sound)
7. T, t	(one horizontal/ vertical stroke)
8. B, b	(shape)
9. P, p	(shape)
0. D, d	(shape)

Even this much is enough for making a system which will do for our day-to-day purpose. For example, to remember **5682310749** we see that the initial letters are CSBNMLDTRP. Can we make some words out of these adding only vowels and neutral letters (i.e. those not used in above system for numbers 1 to 9 and 0). What about COSBY 'N' ME LEAD A TRIP. In fact you could decide that preposition and conjunctions like on, at, or, etc. would not be taken into account for deciphering the sentence. It would make linking different words easy.

However, to make a standardized and fixed system, you can give the numbers fixed words on the above basis and extend it with other fixed numbers.

1	LEG	2	NOAH
3	ME	4	RAG
5	CIA	6	SHE
7	TIE	8	BEE
9	PEA	0	DIE
10	LOAD	11	LILY etc.

Suppose you need to remember a telephone number **562 3187**. The words on the above system could be (either already fixed on the above pattern or being fixed for the first time for this particular problem)—**CUSHION** (562) **MILE** (31) **BOOT** (87). You may imagine a **Cushion**

of air in your boots which are a mile long.

This system can be further developed for card games. We can fix words for both fifty-two cards as well as all the thirteen cards (if necessary for jokers also) in each of the suits.

A practical example of the above method can be to remember the day of the week on which a particular date in the current year would fall. If we know on which date the first Sunday of each month falls we can know all the days for that particular month. So we need to remember only twelve numbers. In the current year 1997, the first Sunday in each month falls on following dates—

5 2 2 6 4 1 6 3 7 5 2 7

We can rearrange them as—

522 641 637 527

If we do not have ready-made words for these numbers from the above system, we can make them now—

CNN	SRL	SMT
CNT	CANON	SURELY
SMOTE	CANT	

You can visualize either a canon of church over coming cant or an army cannon firing at a cantonment.

How powerful the mnemonics system can be illustrated by an example. Suppose we are asked to memorize the value of pie up to 20 decimal points which is—

3.14158265358979323846

In less than ten minutes I came up with—

Pie.

I know a trick limerick to

Easily write its value unending

Perfectly without slightest ado

To the decimals they desire

(The length of each word, i.e. the number of letters in it, correspond to the value at that place: **pie. = 3., I = 1, know = 4, etc.**)

23

LINK THE ITEMS WITH NUMBER-ASSOCIATIONS

Every number has got a strong association with some other thing. We have already seen some of these associations in number-sound and number-shape. Phonetics or number-letter association is also an example of it though this association is somewhat contrived.

In this particular system we take such association as the association of **13** with **bad luck**. As with all above systems here also the system could be developed as per individual associations (for example one could associate a number with the number of one's brothers and sisters). An illustrative association list is given below—

1	=	I
2	=	Parents
3	=	Trinity
4	=	Directions (4th of July)
5	=	Fingers
6	=	Sixer in Cricket (six wickets)
7	=	Lucky number
8	=	Perfect figure
9	=	Cloud nine
10	=	Decimal system
11	=	Jack of cards
12	=	A dozen
13	=	Unlucky number
14	=	Valentine's day
15	=	Half a month
16	=	Sweet sixteen

17	=	Still sweet
18	=	Adult (Adultery)
19	=	Last of teens
20	=	Perfect vision

IV

Tips for Particular Problems

Nothing is good enough if it has no practical applications. All the tips given so far have been studied with reference to general problems and applications. Now we come to the particular applications.

Most vocal regrets about bad memory are expressed with reference to forgetting names and faces, numbers and telephone numbers, and words. Memory is also blamed for poor performance as a speaker and student.

In this Chapter we shall give some hints to combat these

problems. Actually the tips have already been given and this Chapter is only about the application of these tips. But to avoid the necessity of referring back and forth repeatedly, we will repeat them, with suitable changes, and add some new tips as well.

24

NAMES AND FACES

Engrave the Name in the Memory—

i. When introduced to someone make sure you hear the name clearly and distinctly. If necessary ask it to be repeated and spelled. Note down any spelling peculiarities.

ii. Repeat the name in mentally and in the ensuing conversation.

Associate/Link the Name—

iii. Try to associate it with persons of identical names, if already known to you, otherwise with similar names.

iv. Try to associate the name, especially the Christian name, with some word of similar sound.

v. Try to link the name with some peculiar facial feature and exaggerate it.

vi. Try to associate the face with the face of known person of same or similar name.

vii. If the name is long or unfamiliar repeat it time and again so that some association comes to mind or it is broken down into its constituent parts which are more familiar.

For example, if you are introduced to a Miss. Roberta, imagine her to be the wife of your friend Mr. Robert, if one is fat and the other is lean and thin conjure the image of Laurel and Hardy. If Roberta is possessive, think of a "robber".

25

NUMBERS AND TELEPHONE NUMBERS

We have very short memory for numbers. Short both in the sense that we can hardly remember a string of more than four digits and also in the sense that within a short time we could forget it completely.

In a sense it is strange that we have such a short memory for numbers. After all there are only ten numbers. In English there are 26 letters still we remember their different combinations (words). Some other languages have even more letters and the combination of consonants and vowels also complicate things.

So, why we don't remember numbers? One reason may be natural lack of capacity of human mind to remember numbers. But some number experts have fantastic memory for numbers. So, there cannot be any inherent shortcoming in our mind. However, still we naturally feel uncomfortable with numbers. The real reason may be that when digits combine they do not make meaningful numbers in the sense letters make. When letters are combined arbitrarily without making meaningful words we cannot remember them too. So, meaning is very essential in remembering (note that meaning is nothing but vivid association).

So, in remembering numbers we must search some meaning in different combinations of them. This is done through the mnemonics already explained.

26

MAKE MNEMONICS

The best mnemonics for bigger numbers are **Phonetic or Number-Letter System.** However, once this is mastered we must progress to **Number-Association System.** Here also we should try to make association for bigger and bigger combinations of digits—

186000	=	Speed of light
15625	=	Cube of 25
1984	=	Orwell
69	=	Upward dualists or reverse
96	=	Downward dualists or reverse
271969	=	Two lucky men on the moon.

WORDS—

Associate Letter, Word, or its Meaning—

i. Try to associate the meaning of the word with the shape or sound of some individual letter in it.

ii. Associate the meaning with the word in some imaginative way.

iii. Associate the word with some similar word in your mother-tongue, if the word is from some other language.

iv. Break the word into smaller words. Associates the meaning of the smaller words in some imaginative way with the meaning of the longer word.

Know the Derivative of the Word—

v. See the derivative of the word in the dictionary which will make the meaning clearer.

How to remember the French word Rendezvous?

If you have looked into its etymology (source) the French word Rendez-vous, present yourself, and by extension know the meaning **a meeting** or **meeting-place**, you may remember the meaning by noting that in **Rendezvous** two words **rendez** (or French verb rendre) and, **vous** meet (by dropping the hyphen).

27

TALKS AND SPEECHES

Here our aim is not to discuss all the finer points of preparing and delivering a speech but to consider only those points which relate to the aspect of memory.

Be Confident—

i. If thousands of others less qualified than you and some of them even uneducated can do it you could also.

ii. You are giving the talk or speech most probably because you are the senior-most official present (as in official meetings) or you are thought of as some authority on the subject.

So most probably your audience is inferior to you either in official hierarchy or knowledge. In fact, imagine that they are total idiots!

iii. Look into your own past and think of the countless talks and speeches heard by you. As a audience did you really pay any particular attention to what was being said. Did you appreciate the logic and arrangement of the matter. Most probably not. Did anybody really deliver a world changing speech, Never. Most of the speeches heard by you were routine and not particularly brilliant. So, don't think that your audience expects something special from you. So even a very routine one would do (till you become an expert orator!).

iv. Don't lead yourself towards a climax of nervous state. Don't sit there dreading and imagining the announcement of your name, you'r going up to the podium, audience's eyes boring into you, etc. In fact, if you are nervous, keep on thinking of some other pleasant matter so that even the announcement of your name comes as a mild surprise to you. Even in between the speech never think of what you are doing (for example, realising that you are giving a speech may bring on an attack of nervousness) and don't look into the eyes of your audience (till you are comfortable with it!).

Play for Time and Confidence—

v. Unless it is some occasion where you have to directly go to the heart of the matter or score points, starts with routine comments or an anecdote (by the very nature an anecdote is hard to forget and easy to tell).

vi. To gain confidence and time your speech may go on something like this—

"Mr. Chairman . . . (you can go on for some time addressing different persons sitting on the dais ending with ladies and gentlemen).

Today we are gathered here for/on the occasion of . . . (everybody knows it but saying some sentences on it will build your confidence).

The honourable Chairman/previous speakers have said . . . (again playing for time and making up your confidence).

If you have lasted so long you could now say what you have come to say!

Link and Hang Over Pegs—

vii. Memorizing a whole speech is not always the best solution. So, try to make some points and link them up through the method of Phonetic System. Keep that slip handy if you are still nervous. The best way, however, for a speech would be the pegging system linked to your house. You may so link the points of the speech with your front garden, entrance, drawing room, sofa, stairs, study table, and bed etc. that it would be impossible for you to forget it at any place!

Examinations—

A shopping list, a few telephone numbers, names and faces, points for a speech, etc. are good material for committing to the memory easily by above methods but what about serious and lengthy study and writing examination papers.

Surely only lists and numbers would not do.

First important point here to be made is that what could work for small things would surely work for the bigger things also. But, of course, we will have to suitably modify our systems to cater for the new requirement. Here it is.

Preparation for examinations is different from the systems of memory improvement but is intimately linked to it and any book on memory improvement must culminate in a detailed discussion of and hints for success in examination. Examinations are concerned with both learning and then writing in the examination hall what you have learnt within a short span of three hours. Here is how to prepare for an examination—

Reading—

Reading involves both fast reading and slow reading. For examination purpose both readings are necessary. Though speed reading is generally recommended by the populist writers to enable the reader to read as much as possible in the shortest possible time this may not be the best way to prepare for an examination where understanding may be as important as reading as much as possible. Suppose you have to take an examination after one week. The syllabus consists of a single book of 200 pages about a proposed forestation project in a given area. You have four hours (two in the morning, two in the evening) on each of the seven days. Here is your plan of reading—

Know the Context—

Speed read the book once. You should read the book like a novel enjoying it, getting involved with it, having the general feel and coverage of the book. This can be done in two hours but let us give it four hours of the first day. At the end of the first day you would fairly well-know the scope and extent of the project and will have a general idea of the issues involved. Let the mind digest the facts and re-arrange them and be ready for more details.

In **speed reading** we try to read faster by avoiding the followings which are the hallmark of a slow reader—

- **Regression or backward movements of the eye**
- **Short eye-span**
- **Slow perception**
- **Uncoordinated eye movement**
- **Habit of slow reading**
- **Poor anticipation from the context**
- **Poor retention**
- **Poor vocabulary**
- **Poor general knowledge of the subject**

- **Habit of vocalisation or sub-vocalisation**
- **Lack of motivation**
- **Lack of concentration**
- **Lack of interest**

Imprint in the Memory—

Read the book slowly once: Usually it is recommended that the whole should be read in parts and committed to memory. However in memory systems we are not recommending learning by rote but learning by understanding. So, we will first read the whole book again but slowly and critically. We will keep a pencil and dictionary handy. In this reading we read slowly constantly asking ourselves the questions **what, why, when, where, who, how, etc.** We will underline headings, important points, factual points, figures, quotations, etc. **Underlining is a great psychological help. It assures you that you have read something carefully.**

Accordingly mind takes notes of it. Look up the words which are not clear to you in the dictionary. Usually more than 50% of any descriptive book is contextual material which one need not commit to memory for examination purpose. So, after this slow reading you are able to know the contextual material and have also marked all the important facts and figures some of which you may even remember.

Make Mind-Map—

Make notes in your own words: Write only headings and important points. It would be a better idea if instead of using linear line by line note making you use the practice called **Mind-Mapping**. In it notes are made resembling schematic diagrams but not exactly planned like them. From a central point branches are drawn in different directions which represent main points. Further sub-branching may represent sub-points. The Map may not look very presentable but it is a great help in remembering.

Associate—

Associate cue and head words: Now try to memorize your notes, at the same time reading the book so that if very general questions are set up in the examination which do not require exact facts and figures you may still be able to answer. In memorizing keep on writing head words and cue and important words.

Test Your Memory—

Reproduce your notes from memory: This is the fifth day. Now try to reproduce your notes. **You will be surprised how difficult it is to write down what you thought you had committed to memory. However, trying to reproduce from memory your mind will pay extra attention next time to the things which**

you had forgotten. Try to see prepared notes as less as possible. Write again the points which you had forgotten first time.

Signal Importance and Urgency to the Mind—

Special study of important questions: This is the sixth day. You are worried about the important questions now. **So, pay attention to important questions only this day. Reproduce your notes for the important questions from the memory alone. Also, read them from the book because you want to prepare them as best as you could.**

Revise whole book and notes back to forward—Generally it happens that the first few chapters of a book are read more than the last one. So, revise the book with the help of your notes from back to front. Read specially the difficult portions. Write, write, write.

Repeat, Repeat, Repeat—

D-Day: The day of the examination has come. You cannot memorize anything which you could not during the whole year and specially the last week. So only revise, that too very generally. **Speed read the book and your notes. You would note that since by now you know much about the subject, the speed reading is really very fast. Furthermore, since you are highly motivated and focused the retention is also nearly perfect. Take your notes and the book with you to the place of examination but do not try to read all the way. Just relax. The book and notes are with you just for psychological moral boosting. They also serve if the mind suddenly signals you to check some fact which it is not sure about.**

Take the Help of Unconscious Mind—

Answering Questions: Select the questions you know best. Then select the two questions which you want to answer first. Write down main points of both in cue words. Then proceed to answer the first question. **You have given your mind the task of preparing answer to the second question while you are writing the answer to the first! Continue in this way. Always speed-read each answer just written to check for mistakes and additional information which memory brings afresh. Also speed-read the complete answer sheet before handing in the answer sheet.**

V

What about the Diary?

Mnemonics and acronyms have, however, limitations. In the great number and complexity of imagery we may get confused what represents what. Money is supposed to solve all our problems and give us enjoyment but its arrival and the very process of earning it, leaves little time and inclination to enjoy life. Similar may be the case be memory systems. Furthermore, the capacity of human mind is unlimited but it is not meant solely for such chores as memorizing shopping lists. Its functions are higher—as a computer is not meant only for word processing.

Furthermore, the best laid plans of man may go awry. At the eleventh hour we may forget our mnemonics symbols and speech. Keeping a shopping list in mind is so much burden and tension on it. Why not rid it of this unnecessary burden. Written things can be visualised and manipulated better and unfinished tasks carried forward to next day. So,

**Give the Mind a Break—
Keep a Diary—**

While going for meetings keep written brief as well with you. Formal speeches should be written. If not a seasoned speaker, it is a good idea to keep with you the important points of the speech in a list form.

Write down each item of work you intend to do during the day in the diary. The first thing at the start of your working day study it. If there are works to be assigned to others give them their works. Then first dispose of routine and small works which will not take much of your time but considerably shorten your list and take off unnecessary tension from your mind. Then do most difficult (and may be distasteful) job first. Once started you would see that in fact it is not that much difficult. At the end of the day again study your list of works. AND DON'T FORGET THAT BIRTHDAY GIFT FOR YOUR WIFE/HUSBAND!

As said earlier no system of self improvement practised for a limited time could work wonders. The practice should be life long and tailored to individual needs which the individual practising the system could only know best and improvise accordingly. The same goes with this book also. Practice, practice, practice.

LIST OF SOME OF OUR PUBLICATIONS

ENGLISH IMPROVEMENT

G-1	Grammar and Composition
G-2	Boost Your Vocabulary
G-5	Spelling Power Made Easy
G-7	Synonyms and Antonyms
G-8	Idioms and Phrases
G-9	Quotations
G-10	Proverbs
G-11	Common Errors in English
G-19	Dictionary of Idioms and Phrases
G-25	Dictionary of Quotations
G-26	Improve Your English
G-28	Improve Your Vocabulary
G-29	Dictionary of Synonyms and Antonyms
G-33	Common Errors in English
G-34	Improve Your Idioms and Phrases
G-41	Basic English Grammar for Schools
G-45	Dictionary for Proverbs
G-58	How to Write Correct English
G-66	Spoken English
G-67	Better Your English

ESSAY WRITING

G-3	Up-to-date School Essays, Letters and Stories
G-17	School Essays, Letters and Paragraphs
G-18	School Essays, Letters for Juniors
G-30	Selected Essays
G-31	Latest Essays
G-32	160 Essays

G-50 67 Model Essays
G-59 Essays for Seniors
G-71 Advanced Essays for IAS and Other Competitive Exams

LETTER WRITING

G-6 Stolen Love Letters
G-20 Readymade Letters
G-38 Improve Your Business Letters
G-39 How to Write Effective Business Letters
G-40 Readymade Business Letters
G-42 Standard Book of Model Letters
G-44 Lively Love Letters
G-47 How to Write Impressive Business Letters
G-48 Top Winning Letters

G.K., IQ, QUIZS AND PUZZLES

G-78 Goodwill's Book of General Knowledge
G-16 Test Your I.Q.
G-22 Check Your I.Q.
G-23 How to Improve Your I.Q.
G-24 I.Q. for All
G-27 Better Your I.Q.
G-51 World Facts at a Glance
G-35 G.K. Quiz
G-52 Do you Know?
G-54 India Quiz
G-56 1250 Questions and Answers Quiz Book
G-57 Super Quiz Book
G-62 Sports Quiz Book
G-68 Science Quiz
G-74 Readymade Quizzes (Foreign Reprint)
G-75 Standard Quiz Book (Foreign Reprint)

G-86 Puzzles for High I.Q. (Foreign Reprint)
G-87 Critical Thinking Puzzles (Foreign Reprint)
G-92 250 Challenging Puzzles

MISCELLANEOUS

G-4 How to Pass Exams
G-37 The Book of Etiquette
G-46 Goodwill's Book of Baby Names
G-49 Readymade Speeches for All Occasions
G-85 4500 Baby Names
G-53 Noble Thoughts for Better Living
G-55 Perfect Public Speaking
G-65 Astrology for All
G-70 The World's Great Speeches
G-60 Common Sexual Problems
G-81 Management—It's Lighter and Brighter Sides
G-80 Power of Positive Doing (Foreign Reprint)
G-84 How to Have a Well Mannered Dog (Foreign Reprint)
G-88 101 Classic Magic Tricks
G-89 Karate Made Easy (Foreign Reprint)

CHEIRO'S

G-90 Cheiro's Guide to the Hand
G-91 Palmistry for All
G-93 Cheiro's Language of the Hand

SELF LEARNING LANGUAGE SERIES

G-60 Learn English from Hindi
G-61 Learn Hindi from English

JOKES

G-12 Top Party Jokes
G-13 1001 Jokes

G-14 Bachelors' Jokes
G-15 Childrens' Jokes
G-21 Lovers' Jokes

TITLES ON CHESS

G-76 First Moves (How to Start a Chess Game) (Foreign Reprint)
G-77 Pick Up the Best Chess Problems (Foreign Reprint)
G-79 Basics and Laws of Chess
G-82 White to Play and Mate in Two (Foreign Reprint)

HEALTH AND FITNESS

G-36 Improve Your Eyesight
G-63 Nature-Cure for Common Diseases
G-64 High Blood Pressure
G-83 100% Fitness (Foreign Reprint)

OBJECTIVE SERIES

G-72 Comprehensive Objective Botany
G-73 Comprehensive Objective Zoology